Religion in the Renaissance

LIZANN FLATT

Crabtree Publishing
www.crabtreebooks

Renaissance World

Author: Lizann Flatt
Editor-in-Chief: Lionel Bender
Editor: Simon Adams
Project coordinator: Kathy Middleton
Photo research: Susannah Jayes
Design concept: Robert MacGregor
Designer: Ben White
Production coordinator: Ken Wright
Production: Kim Richardson
Prepress technician: Ken Wright

Consultant: Lisa Mullins, Department of History and
Philosophy of Science, University of Cambridge

Cover photo: The Adoration of the Shepherds
by Lorenzo di Credi
Photo credit: © Arte & Immagini srl/CORBIS

Photographs and reproductions:
The Granger Collection, NYC/TopFoto: pages 1, 5, 7, 12, 15,
16, 17, 18, 20, 21, 22, 24, 25, 26, 27, 30, 31
iStockphoto.com: pages 4, 9, 10, 11, 14
Topfoto: pages 6 (Roger-Viollet/TopFoto), 8 (Print Collector/
HIP/TopFoto), 13 (Topham Picturepoint), 19 (Topham
Picturepoint), 23 (Topham Picturepoint), 28 (TopFoto.co.uk),
29 (Hubertus Kanus/Topfoto)

Photo on page 1: An oil painting by Juan de Valdes Leal of
Ignatius Loyola receiving the approval of the Society of
Jesus's constitution from Pope Paul III.

This book was produced for Crabtree Publishing Company by
Bender Richardson White

Library and Archives Canada Cataloguing in Publication
Flatt, Lizann
    Religion in the Renaissance / Lizann Flatt.
(Renaissance world) Includes index.
ISBN 978-0-7787-4597-6 (bound).--ISBN 978-0-7787-4617-1
(pbk.)
    1. Church history--Middle Ages, 600-1500--Juvenile litera-
ture. 2. Church history--16th century--Juvenile literature.
3. Europe--Church history--Juvenile literature. 4. Reformation--
Juvenile literature. 5. Renaissance--Juvenile literature.
6. Catholic Church--Influence--Juvenile literature.
I. Title. II. Series: Renaissance world (St. Catharines, Ont.)

BR280.F53 2010   j274'.05   C2009-902429-2

Library of Congress Cataloging-in-Publication Data
Flatt, Lizann.
    Religion in the Renaissance / Lizann Flatt.
        p. cm. -- (Renaissance world) Includes index.
    ISBN 978-0-7787-4617-1 (pbk. : alk. paper) -- ISBN 978-0-
7787-4597-6 (reinforced library bdg. : alk. paper)
    1. Church history--Middle Ages, 600-1500--Juvenile litera-
ture. 2. Church history--16th century--Juvenile literature. 3.
Europe--Church history--Juvenile literature. 4. Reformation--
Europe--Juvenile literature. 5. Renaissance--Juvenile litera-
ture. 6. Catholic Church--Influence--Juvenile literature. I.
Title. II. Series.
    BR280.F53 2009
    274'.06--dc22
                                                    2009016729

Crabtree Publishing Company
www.crabtreebooks.com   1-800-387-7650

Published in Canada
Crabtree Publishing
616 Welland Ave.
St. Catharines, Ontario
L2M 5V6

Published in the United States
Crabtree Publishing
PMB16A
350 Fifth Ave., Suite 3308
New York, NY 10118

Published in the United Kingdom
Crabtree Publishing
White Cross Mills
High Town, Lancaster
LA1 4XS

Published in Australia
Crabtree Publishing
386 Mt. Alexander Rd.
Ascot Vale (Melbourne)
VIC 3032

Contents

The Renaissance

During the Renaissance the Christian religion in western Europe underwent a huge and lasting change. At the start of the Renaissance, there was only one acceptable way to practice Christianity. By the end of the Renaissance, there were several different Christian religions.

The Renaissance

The European Renaissance was a period of time between about 1300 to the early 1600s. The term "Renaissance" means "rebirth" in French. During this time, scholars and artists looked back more than 1,000 years to the ideas and discoveries in the literature, art, science, architecture, and politics of ancient Greece and Rome. Italy was the first country to experience this rebirth, which later spread to the rest of Europe. During the Renaissance, new lands were discovered, the development of the printing press helped spread new ideas, and the discovery of gunpowder led to the creation of deadlier weapons. It was a time of great change in the way people lived their lives, in the way they related to their church, and in the way they thought about their religion.

The Gutenberg Bible

In the 1450s, the development of the printing press and moveable type by the German goldsmith, Johannes Gutenberg, meant that a book could be quickly printed hundreds of times rather than copied out individually by hand. The Bible, the book of Christian teachings, was one of the first books to be printed on this revolutionary machine. Produced between 1453 and 1455, this edition of the Bible became known as the Gutenberg Bible. Only 180 copies were printed, and very few complete copies still exist today. It was printed in Latin, the language of the Church and scholars.

The island of San Georgio Maggiore, Venice, is the site of a Benedictine **monastery.** *Beside the monastery is the Roman Catholic Church of St. Georgio Maggiore, begun in 1566 and which is still run by Benedictine monks today.*

What is Religion?

A **religion** is an organized system of faith and beliefs. It usually involves a set of teachings about a superior being or creator, although some religions believe in many gods. Followers of a religion worship, or show respect to, the deity in a specified way.

At the start of the Renaissance, most people in Europe were Christians and followed the teachings of Jesus Christ. At this time, being a Christian meant being a member of either the Roman Catholic or the Orthodox Church. These two Christian Churches had split from one another in 1054. In eastern Europe, Russia, Greece, and western Asia, Orthodox Christians generally looked to the patriarch in Constantinople to lead their Church. In western Europe, Roman Catholics looked to the pope in Rome as their leader.

By the end of the Renaissance, the Protestant Reformation had swept through Europe. Some people wanted to reform the Catholic Church, but the Church resisted. This led to a new type of Christian faith called Protestantism. The Protestant faith is actually made up of many different Churches. Protestants got their name from a group of German princes who "protested" when the Catholic Church took back its agreement to let them practice their new religion.

*Dominican monk Johann Tetzel leads a procession through a German town in 1517 offering **indulgences** for sale, a practice that caused Martin Luther to protest.*

TIMELINE

1309–77: Babylonian Captivity, when popes live in Avignon

1347–50: First outbreak of the bubonic plague or Black Death

1378–1417: Great Schism, when two popes claim the title

1382: Bible first translated into English by John Wycliffe and followers

1455: Gutenberg Bible printed

1517: Martin Luther writes his 95 Theses

1523: Luther translates New Testament into German

1534: King Henry VIII makes himself head of the church in England

1536 John Calvin publishes first edition of *Institutes of the Christian Religion*

1555: Holy Roman Empire officially recognizes the Lutheran Church

1559: Queen Elizabeth I establishes Church of England

1562–98: Huguenot wars in France

1604 King James I of England authorizes translation of the Bible into English

1618–48: Thirty Years' War in Holy Roman Empire

1626: St Peter's basilica consecrated in Rome

1648: Peace of Westphalia recognizes the existence of the Catholic, Lutheran, and Calvinist Churches

The Religious World

The Catholic Church dominated religion in western Europe at the start of the Renaissance, but the growth of **humanism** and the outbreak of the plague began to affect how people viewed religion.

Religious Regions

At the beginning of the Renaissance, Roman Catholicism was the dominant religion of western Europe. Jews, the people who practice Judaism, were scattered in cities all over Europe. Muslims, the people who practice Islam, lived in northern Africa, southern Spain, southeast Europe, and the Middle East. These areas were mostly controlled by the vast Ottoman Empire. The Ottomans were Muslims from Turkey, but they allowed Orthodox Christians and Jews within their empire to practice their own religion without any interference.

A tithe barn from Parçay-Meslay in France. Tithe barns and buildings were constructed to store the crops and produce people gave to the Church each year as a tithe, or tax.

The Tithe

Within Europe the Catholic Church owned and controlled much land. The Church earned money from that land and its people in the form of a **tithe**. This was a **tax** consisting of one-tenth of a person's income or one-tenth of the crops they produced or the animals they reared on their land. This tax was used by the Church to support the **clergy,** help the poor, and maintain its buildings. Peasants and nobles alike had to contribute to the Church. If they did not, they could be **excommunicated**, or cut off from the Church. This was a serious threat, because it meant that the person had no hope of going to heaven after death and would face eternal punishment and damnation in hell.

Humanism

A new movement called humanism developed during the Renaissance. This movement believed in the value of humans and in the achievements of **classical** Greece and Rome. While studying classical manuscripts, Renaissance scholars discovered that the original texts were different than the translations used and taught by the Church. This caused some people to question whether belief in the Church's teachings was the only way to be a good Christian.

Plague

The **bubonic plague** was a deadly disease caused by a bacterium that was spread by rats and their fleas. The first outbreak of plague happened late in 1347 and lasted until about 1350. The plague caused high fever, aching limbs, and swollen lymph glands in the neck, armpit, and groin. These glands were called buboes, which is where the name bubonic plague comes from. The disease also caused blackening of the skin, so it came to be called the Black Death. It would kill a person in three to four days. The plague killed 20 to 30 million people, nearly one in three in Europe.

Peasants, princes, and the clergy were all infected. With so much death everywhere people began to question why God had not answered their prayers and ended the plague. Some said it was a punishment sent by God. Survivors wondered why they were spared when others were not. The plague caused people to question their faith as never before.

Church Hierarchy

Members of the church organization are called the clergy. A deacon is training to become a priest, and assists the priest. A priest is the head of his church and the region or parish surrounding it. A bishop looks after a diocese, an area made up of many parishes. An archbishop controls an archdiocese, a larger area made up of several dioceses, and is head of all the bishops in his archdiocese. A cardinal is a bishop chosen by the pope to be one of his main advisors. When a pope dies or resigns the cardinals meet in Rome and elect a new pope. The pope is the head of the entire Roman Catholic Church and the bishop of Rome.

A doctor lances a bubo on a patient infected with the plague. Unfortunately, this practice did not cure the illness, and the patient died.

A Religious Life

Religion was part of everyday life for rich and poor. At the start of the Renaissance, nearly everyone was a Roman Catholic.

Part of Life

The Roman Catholic Church was an essential part of everyday life. It performed the rituals that were central to all stages of life. The Church baptized children when they were born, performed marriages, and then buried people when they died. The Church looked after the sick and the poor. People attended a church service called mass on Sundays, and special holy days, at their local church. At mass the community gathered to pray and give thanks to God. Passages from the Bible were read aloud and a priest gave a sermon. The service was in Latin, a language few people understood, but the sermon was in the everyday language of the people.

Sin

Christians believed that any wrongdoing such as lying or stealing was a sin that broke God's law. People needed to free themselves of sin because they believed that after death the soul would carry on, going to either heaven, hell, or **purgatory**. Hell was a place of eternal suffering for sinners. Heaven was a place of eternal joy with God for those who had been faithful and were cleansed of sin.

Purgatory was where a soul who was destined for heaven went first to suffer, for as many as 1,000 years, in order to be purified or cleansed of sin before being allowed into heaven. Time in purgatory could be shortened by doing good works during your life, going on a **pilgrimage** to the Holy Land, or by having the living pray for your soul after your death.

During the plague, some Christians called flagellants took up the practice of publicly whipping themselves because they believed they would receive God's forgiveness this way. The Church banned this practice in 1349 and arrested or put to death many of them.

Confession and Indulgences

Confessing sins to a priest, and then doing a task to do penance or make up for the sin, helped to free a soul of sin. Indulgences were pieces of paper sold by the Church that signified the purchaser had atoned for his or her sin by supporting the Church's good works instead of performing his or her own. Selling indulgences made the Church a lot of money.

Clergy

Only men could become priests. A man could also become a monk and live in a monastery, while a woman could become a nun and live in a convent. Both had to take vows to never marry or have children, to live in poverty, and to spend their lives in prayer, work, and study. They lived their lives mostly without direct contact with the outside world, although some monks did charity work for the poor. Some nuns ran hospitals that were attached to the convent. A friar is a member of a religious order, the biggest of which were the Dominicans or Franciscans. Friars lived and worked in the outside world, teaching, preaching, and hearing confessions.

A confessional inside a cathedral, where a person privately confesses their sins to a priest. The priest forgives the sin on behalf of God and assigns a task, such as prayer or a specific action, to atone for the sin. This process is called penance and is one of the sacred ceremonies of the Catholic Church.

Saints and Relics

A saint is someone formally recognized by the Church as having done something important for their faith, such as performing miracles or keeping their beliefs in the face of extreme hardship. A relic could be a bone from the saint's body or something they once owned. Some people believed that saints' relics had the power to cure the sick or work miracles. Relics were stored in churches, usually in elaborate boxes called reliquaries. People prayed to the saints and asked them to intervene on their behalf to God.

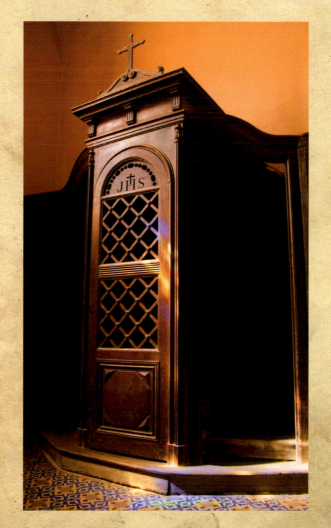

The Renaissance Cathedral

The cathedral was the church of a bishop. Many were large because most bishops lived in a city and had the means to raise enough money to build large cathedrals.

New Approach

The Renaissance approach to cathedral design was to create a place where people felt surrounded by God rather than have God soaring above them, as was created with the earlier style of Gothic architecture.

Cathedrals were built with an emphasis on **horizontal** lines, rather than vertical lines that pointed toward the sky. The use of **perspective** was also important, and columns or arches in the foreground were used to frame an important element in the background, such as a doorway or altar.

To Renaissance architects, the ideal cathedral had a circular floor plan because a circle was seen as a perfect shape and so perfect like God. In reality, this plan was often modified to one in the shape of a Greek cross, where all four arms of the cross are of equal length. The open space in the center, where the arms met, was capped with a high dome. The Church mainly favored the Latin cross, or basilican plan, where the arms are shorter than the upright, because smaller church services could go on in side chapels at the same time as the service at the main altar. In the Renaissance style, the main aisle or nave had a flat ceiling and a series of columns and arches that directed attention to the altar, the most important part of the church.

The cathedral of Jaen in Spain, built in 1540, shows the main Renaissance architectural features of giant columns, regularly spaced rows of windows, and statues placed in niches, or double columns emphasize the center of the building and the doorway.

Inside a Cathedral

The altar was usually placed under the main dome. The bishop's throne sat to the side of the altar. A large cathedral could have more than one altar and many separate chapels in which to worship. Some cathedrals had chapels with a special purpose, such as the baptistery, where baptisms were performed. Others had chambers for priests to put on their robes and offices for the clergy. Decorations inside the cathedral were numerous. Statues of Biblical figures were placed in niches or recesses along the walls. Frescoes, or paintings created on wet plaster, decorated the interior of a cathedral's dome and walls. Paintings, **altarpieces,** and stained-glass windows showed scenes from the Bible. This helped people who could not read to understand their stories.

The church of Santa Maria Novella in Florence, Italy. Designed by architect Leon Battista Alberti, the black and white marble tiles were arranged in geometric patterns to give the building a look of proportion and harmony.

Starting a Style

Filippo Brunelleschi is said to have started the Renaissance style in the dome he built over the Florence Cathedral between 1420 and 1436. The eight-sided dome soars 348 feet (106 meters) above the street and is 138 feet (42 meters) across. He went on to design several more churches and buildings in Florence, including a hospital. In addition to being an architect, Brunelleschi was a trained and skilled goldsmith and sculptor and was admired for his abilities in many different areas.

Religion in Art

Religious themes in art were very important during the Renaissance. By paying an artist to create a religious piece to decorate a church, believers could accumulate good works to reduce their time in purgatory.

New Style

Renaissance artists found inspiration in the Bible and used its stories as subjects for painting and sculpture. Under the influence of humanism, religious characters were now shown with real human emotions. Artists studied anatomy so that they portrayed the human body and its muscles realistically. Body proportions, such as how big the head should be in relation to the body, were also correct. Perspective was used to make characters or the setting recede into the background, so that the figures in the front were larger than those in the back. Before this, artists made the most important figure in the painting the one who was the largest, regardless of where they stood in the picture.

Art on Display

Frescoes of Bible scenes decorated the interior walls, domes, and ceilings of churches and cathedrals. Altarpieces on the panel or wall behind the altar were also elaborately decorated with Biblical stories or themes. Doors to churches featured bronze sculptures or wood carvings. Tombs featured sculptures of Christian saints and the Virgin Mary but also elements from classical times, such as mythological figures and garlands, scrolls, and columns. Spaces above doorways or windows might also feature carvings. Religious pieces were also displayed in public spaces. Michelangelo's David, the young man who defeated a giant in the Bible story, was placed in Florence's main **piazza**.

This story of Joseph created by Lorenzo Ghiberti is one of the panels on the bronze baptistery doors of Florence Cathedral. The sculpture gives a great sense of depth so that it seems as if the figures are in front of the curved building and that other buildings are receding into the background behind it.

Popes as Patrons

Popes were patrons of many great artists. Pope Julius II commissioned or hired Michelangelo to paint a fresco on the ceiling of the Sistine Chapel. Michelangelo did not want to do it, preferring to work in sculpture. He also had a disagreement with the pope about overdue payments. He agreed to do the work and painted it standing on scaffolding about 70 feet (21 meters) high. The ceiling, showing the creation of the world, was finished in 1512. Michelangelo wrote a poem about the discomfort of having to strain his neck and getting paint splashed in his face while he worked on the ceiling. Pope Paul III commissioned Michelangelo for another fresco, *The Last Judgment,* for the altar wall. Michelangelo depicted many nudes in the scene, which caused controversy when it as unveiled. The nudes were later covered up.

In the Picture

Artists were hired to produce religious paintings, sculptures, or other works of art by a patron. This was a wealthy person who wanted to show off their wealth and to create good works on earth to reduce their time in purgatory. Putting an altarpiece in a church or sponsoring a church decoration was an outward sign of how pious they were, and would serve them well as they faced an afterlife of either heaven or hell.

Patrons often paid to have themselves put into a religious scene to show their piety. Lorenzo de' Medici commissioned Alessandro Botticelli to paint the Biblical scene where the three magi give gifts to the baby Jesus at his birth. The magi appear as Lorenzo and his relatives Cosimo and Giuiliano de' Medici.

Michelangelo's Pieta *shows Christ after his death in his mother Mary's arms. The marble sculpture is noted for the details in the graceful folds of cloth, the natural position of Jesus's limbs, and the quiet restraint and dignity of the figures.*

Popes and Power

The pope is the head of the Roman Catholic Church. During the Renaissance he held great power, but splits in the Church and the fact that some popes neglected spiritual matters caused confusion for the Church's followers.

The Avignon Popes

The pope held ultimate authority in the Church. He was the bishop of Rome, the ruler of the **Papal States** in Italy, and appointed all the cardinals. These cardinals elected a new pope when the old pope died. In 1304 the cardinals elected a French pope, Clement V. In 1309 Clement decided to move to Avignon in France to get away from the rivalry of the cardinals in Rome. He intended this to be a temporary move, but subsequent popes remained there, giving the French king influence over the pope. People did not like the pope being away from Rome, so Gregory XI finally agreed to return in 1377.

The Great Schism

After Gregory XI died in 1378, the French cardinals elected an Italian, Urban VI, as pope, hoping to please the citizens of Rome, but he brought in reforms to cut down the wealth of the cardinals. In response, the French cardinals said the election was not valid because they had been pressured into casting their votes, so they elected a new French pope, Clement VII, who went back to Avignon. For the next 39 years, there was one pope in Avignon and another in Rome. This confused followers and shook their faith in the Church itself. In 1409 a group of clergy tried to solve things by electing a new pope, but that only made things worse by creating a third pope. Finally, the **Holy Roman Emperor** gathered the leading clergymen from across Europe. They removed two popes and the third resigned. A single new Italian pope, Martin V, was elected in 1417.

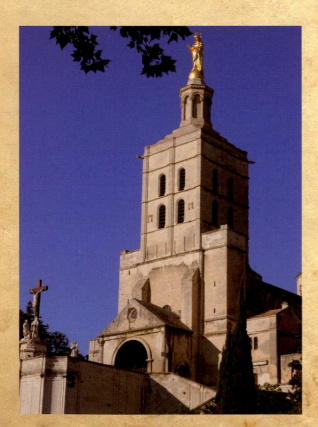

Palais des Papes in Avignon, France, where Pope Clement V moved in 1309. It was the only residence of the popes until 1377 and home to one of the two popes until 1417.

Excesses and Individuals

After the Great Schism, or split, the rule of most of the Renaissance popes continued to erode people's faith in the Church. Many popes were members of prominent Italian families. They spent much time and money as patrons of the arts and seemed more concerned with political power than with the spiritual concerns of the Church. At this time, a pope could appoint anyone to be a cardinal, even someone who was not a member of the clergy. Pope Sixtus IV (elected 1471) appointed three of his nephews as cardinals. He got involved in the plot to murder Florence's ruler, Lorenzo de' Medici, and his brother. Pope Alexander VI (1492) lived defiantly with his mistress, had several children, and got involved in political conspiracies. Pope Julius II (1503) was involved in several wars, including one against Venice, and had an illegitimate daughter. Pope Leo X (1513) was the second son of Lorenzo de' Medici and he too appointed his relatives to positions of power.

This fresco by Vasari shows Pope Clement VII marrying Catherine de' Medici, his niece, to the future Henry II of France in 1533. Clement VII, born Giulio de' Medici, was himself appointed a cardinal by his cousin Pope Leo X, the son of Lorenzo de' Medici.

Papal Bulls

Popes could issue a bull, or a statement, on paper that formally declared their wishes. A bull was meant to be obeyed by everyone. In 1303 Pope Boniface VIII issued a bull called the *Unam sanctam*. He was quarreling with the king of France, Philip IV, who had arrested a bishop and demanded taxes from Church officials. This threatened the Church's authority in France. The bull said that, in order to go to heaven, all humans had to submit to the authority of the pope in both civil and religious matters. This made Philip so angry that his army marched into Italy and imprisoned the pope for three days. Boniface died shortly afterward.

The Holy Roman Empire

The Holy Roman Empire was a huge territory centered in Germany that was ruled by an emperor and contained many smaller states, each one ruled by a prince. The Empire had traditionally accepted the pope as ruler in spiritual matters while the emperor ran the government.

The Empire

At the start of the Renaissance, the Holy Roman Empire included Germany, Austria, Belgium, the Netherlands, the Czech lands of Bohemia, and parts of France and Italy. Because of its close ties to the Church, the Empire was considered a Catholic nation with Catholic rulers.

The emperor was elected by German princes and crowned by the pope, but there were often struggles between the pope and emperor over who had authority over the other. In 1338 Emperor Louis IV and the German princes declared that the pope's acceptance of the elected emperor was not necessary. This angered the pope, who deposed Louis and created Charles of Luxembourg as Emperor Charles IV. The pope's choice was not accepted by the German nobles until 1346, when Louis died and Charles took over. Conflicts also erupted between the emperor and his German nobles, resulting in civil war. At the start of the Renaissance, these conflicts took up much of the emperor's attention and left the Empire's lands in Italy to largely govern themselves.

Holy Roman Emperor Charles IV arrives in Paris to visit his nephew, King Charles V of France, in 1378. This family connection meant that the Empire and France were at peace during their reigns.

The Habsburgs

In 1438 Albert II of the Austrian Habsburg family was elected Holy Roman Emperor. By using family marriages to create alliances, the Habsburg family became related to most royal families in Europe and gained great power in the Empire. As a result, the Habsburgs held on to the Empire, passing the imperial crown down from father to son.

Maximilian I, a Habsburg, became emperor in 1493. He too arranged marriages for his children to help secure the family's influence over the Empire. With the Empire's ties to Rome, this also meant that the influence of the Catholic Church remained strong. His son, Philip, married Joanna, daughter of the king and queen of Spain. Their son, Charles, became ruler of the Netherlands and Burgundy in 1506, king of Spain as Charles I in 1516, and ruler of the Habsburg lands and Holy Roman Emperor with the title Charles V in 1519. The Empire's influence reached its peak during Charles V's reign. He controlled more territory than any king in Europe, with all of Spain and its lands in the Americas as well as the Empire itself. Charles, however, faced Protestant turmoil at home, pressure from the Ottoman empire to the east, and war with France for territory in Italy.

By 1556 he had divided his empire between his son, Philip II, and his brother, Ferdinand I. He then retired to a monastery, where he died in 1558.

Portrait by Bernhard Strigel of Holy Roman Emperor Maximilian I, his son Philip, his wife Mary, his grandsons Ferdinand I and Charles V, and his granddaughter Mary's husband, Louis II of Hungary.

Expansion with Explorers

In 1517 Ferdinand Magellan asked Emperor Charles V to sponsor a voyage west to Asia by way of South America and the Pacific Ocean. Charles agreed because the Portuguese controlled the eastern route to Asia around Africa. If Magellan was successful, Spain would have its own route to Asia. Magellan was killed on the journey, but his crew reached Spain on September 6, 1522, after completing the first trip around the world.

Calls for Change

During the Renaissance, religious men called for change and reform within the Church. While they did not always succeed, their ideas were used by later reformers who were successful.

The Lollards

John Wycliffe, a professor and priest in England, believed the Church was too wealthy and said people should not pay their tithes. He and his followers translated the Bible into English in 1382. Wycliffe believed that all people should be able to read the Bible. He translated many religious texts into English. People who believed his teachings were called Lollards. The Church declared them **heretics** in the early 1400s and some were burned at the stake. The Lollard movement died out, but it greatly influenced the priest John Hus, who preached similar ideas in Bohemia. The Church excommunicated him and he was burned at the stake in 1415.

Bonfire of the Vanities

Girolamo Savonarola, an Italian priest, preached sermons in Florence against the clergy, the papacy, bankers, humanists, and some of their art and literature. In 1496 he sent groups of young boys around the city to gather offerings for the poor during the carnival. The next year he had these groups go from house to house gathering anything he considered immoral, such as mirrors, perfume, fancy clothing, wigs, and jewelry. These things were taken to the piazza, piled in a heap, and set on fire in the "bonfire of the vanities." Savonarola was criticized by citizens who did not like his ban on taverns and gambling, and by clergy who resented his criticisms. Pope Alexander VI was angered by his attacks on the papacy and excommunicated Savonarola in 1497. He was arrested, tortured, and burned at the stake.

Lollards, followers of John Wycliffe, toured the English countryside reading the Bible to people in their own language, so that for the first time they could hear what the Bible said. At this time, the Church clergy read the Bible only in Latin, a language few people understood.

Christian Humanism

In northern Europe humanists were often called Christian humanists because of their emphasis on studying religious documents. They studied classical Greek and Latin so they could better understand the Bible in its original words. From this work they discovered differences among the various translations of the Bible that led them to question some of the Church's practices.

Dutch scholar Desiderius Erasmus was the best known of these critics. In 1503 he wrote *Handbook of a Christian Soldier*, in which he stressed morality, piety, and dedication to truth. He criticized the clergy for neglecting these values and for their emphasis on placing ceremonies and church law above those values.

Erasmus pointed out that the religious practices the Church claimed were essential for salvation were not how the original followers of Christ practiced Christianity. He produced the Bible's New Testament in Greek, making the original text available for the first time in 1516. He then translated that Greek version into Latin.

Saint Thomas More

Thomas More was a famous Christian humanist, a friend of Erasmus, and an official in Henry VIII's government in England. More wrote *Utopia*, about a society where there was justice and equality for all. When More refused to swear that the king of England had authority over the pope, he was beheaded for treason in 1535. The Catholic Church declared him a saint in 1935 and made him the patron saint of statesmen and politicians in 2000.

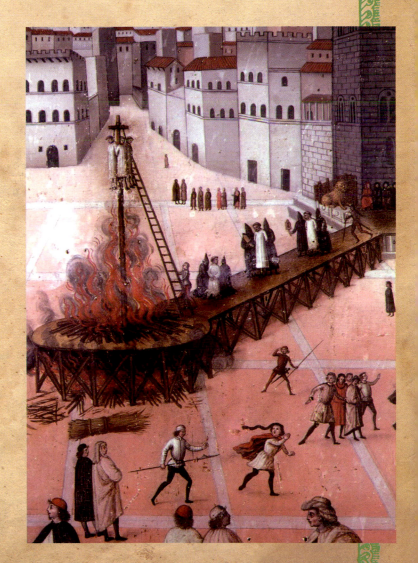

This painting shows the death of Girolamo Savonarola. Savonarola and two of his followers were hanged and burned on May 23, 1498 in the Piazza della Signoria, or town square, of Florence, Italy.

The Protestant Reformation

Martin Luther established a new branch of Christianity, separate from the Catholic Church, called Protestantism. Luther's followers, called Lutherans, were the first Protestants, but the Protestant movement itself established several new churches.

Lutheranism

Martin Luther was a monk but he was very critical of the luxury some bishops lived in. He disagreed with the Church's practice of selling **bishoprics** and indulgences to raise money for building projects. Luther believed that people needed faith, that God alone could grant salvation to one's soul, and that good works did not guarantee salvation. This was completely contrary to the Church's claim that doing good works and following the sacraments were necessary for salvation.

Luther wrote his 95 Theses, or statements against the sale of indulgences, in 1517. Printed copies spread rapidly throughout Germany. His teachings gathered a following known as Lutherans, and his church became the Lutheran Church. In 1521 Pope Leo X excommunicated him and declared him a heretic. Emperor Charles V declared him an outlaw, which meant anyone could kill him without punishment, but his supporters helped him escape and hid him.

Calvinism

In Geneva, Switzerland, another form of Protestantism began under John Calvin. He was a Lutheran and studied the Bible, but he believed in a literal translation so that anything not specifically mentioned in the Bible was to be rejected and anything specifically mentioned was to be followed literally. In 1536 he published *Institutes of the Christian Religion*, which set out his beliefs.

Martin Luther was an ordained priest and professor of theology. He did not set out to start a new church, just to reform the established one. Luther also wrote hymns and believed the congregation should sing in a church service.

The Calvinist Church

Under Calvin's leadership, strict practices were put into effect in Geneva, including getting up early, working hard, having good morals, avoiding worldly pleasures, and being thrifty, sober, and serious. He believed that people were helpless before an all-powerful God, that there was no such thing as free will, and that individuals were **predestined** to go to either heaven or hell. Only people called the Elect would be saved and only God knew who they were. Good works were an outward sign that someone was making the best of their time on Earth, but they did not guarantee salvation.

Calvinist ministers traveled throughout Europe organizing new groups. By Calvin's death in 1564, Calvinism had a serious following in Scotland, the Netherlands, Hungary, and France. In France, they were known as Huguenots.

Dividing the Empire

In 1555 the Protestant princes of the Holy Roman Empire forced Charles V to accept the Treaty of Augsburg. This allowed each Lutheran or Roman Catholic prince to choose which faith his land would follow. It also divided the Empire's church lands between the two faiths. This treaty gave Lutheran churches equal status with the Roman Catholic Church, but did not recognize the Calvinist and other Protestant groups and created much conflict later.

*John Calvin developed a form of church government where all ministers have equal rank. A board made up of the minister and **lay** elders run each church, which in turn sends representatives to higher church councils that govern larger districts. This is called the presbyterian system of church government.*

Henry VIII's Church

England's split with the Roman Catholic Church was motivated more by politics than matters of faith. King Henry VIII declared himself the head of the church in England because the pope would not annul, or cancel, his first marriage. He wanted to remarry because his first wife had not produced any male heirs to the throne. As head of the church, he annulled his own marriage and then married again.

The Counter – Reformation

With so many people leaving the Catholic Church for the Protestant churches, the Roman Catholic Church began its own reforms. It formed new societies of monks to keep its following and to bring others back to the faith. This is called either the Catholic or the Counter-Reformation.

Ignatius Loyola, a soldier who became a monk, receives the approval of Pope Paul III in 1540 for the Jesuits' constitution. The Catholic Church declared Loyola a saint in 1622 for his efforts on behalf of the faith.

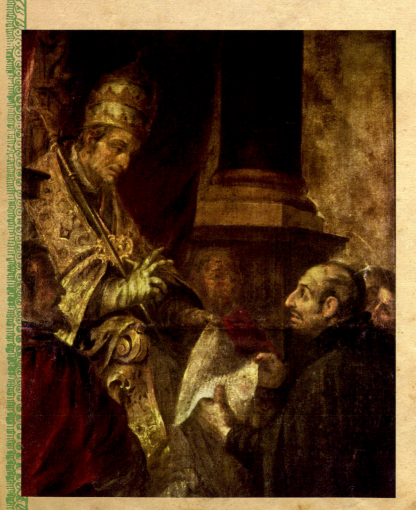

The Jesuits

The Society of Jesus, or the Jesuit order of monks, was formed in 1534 by Ignatius Loyola and six other men. Loyola wanted this new religious order to be free of any bishops or established Church hierarchy, so that he could avoid any association with corruption. He preached that there was no predestination, a main belief of the Protestant faiths, and that people should have hope in their salvation because of the power of a priest to offer forgiveness. Jesuits believed that the Church had authority in all matters of faith and swore special obedience to the pope. They promoted religious education and founded many schools. Many Jesuits became **missionaries** and went to preach Christianity in the Americas and Asia.

The Capuchins

The Order of Friars Minor Capuchin, or Capuchins, was a new branch of Franciscan monks founded in 1525 by Friar Matteo da Bascio. They believed in simplicity and poverty, begging for food and going barefoot. Capuchin friars hoped to impress the peasants and the poor and **convert** or keep them Catholic through their own strict poverty, plain living, and preaching. Their name comes from the capuche, or pointed hood, they wore.

Council of Trent

A series of 25 meetings held between 1545 and 1563 in Trent, Italy became known as the Council of Trent. The council was begun by Pope Paul III to define Catholic beliefs and address some of the criticisms the Protestants had directed at the Church. The council restated that the Church was the only authority for interpreting the Bible, and rejected the Protestant views of sin and salvation. The council also defined the importance of the **sacraments**, defended the granting of indulgences, and approved the practice of praying to saints.

The council created new requirements that each bishop live in his diocese and visit his parishes. It forbade the practice of selling bishoprics and other positions in the church, and encouraged the building of **seminaries** in every diocese to train priests. A catechism, a written instruction on religion, was published consisting of a series of questions and answers on Catholic religious beliefs, as well as books on the rituals of worship so there would be more standardization of practices within the Church. The council also reestablished the Inquisition to fight the spread of Protestantism.

An oil painting by Titian of the Council of Trent in session. The decisions made at these meetings were confirmed by Pope Pius IV on January 26, 1564 and influenced Church practices until the mid-20th century.

New Schools

As part of the Counter-Reformation movement the Roman Catholic Church increased its educational activities. Several Catholic monastic orders established local schools for Catholic children that would teach them in their own languages.

These schools gave the children a basic education but also taught them the essentials of Catholic morality and beliefs. Protestant churches established their own schools with the same goal of teaching children the Protestant faith and morality.

The Inquisition

The Inquisition was set up by the Catholic Church to find and get rid of people it considered heretics, including Protestants, witches, and those who followed other religions.

Spanish Inquisition

The first modern inquisition was set up in Spain. In 1478 King Ferdinand and Queen Isabella established the Supreme Council of the Inquisition with papal approval. They wanted to expose Jews who had pretended to convert to Christianity. In the early 1500s the Inquisition also looked for those who had pretended to convert from Islam, |as well as any Protestants, as they were felt to be a danger to the Church and to the country. The papacy gave up supervision of this inquisition to the Spanish monarchy, so it became a tool for the state. About 2,000 people were burned at the stake.

The Congregation

In 1542 the Roman Catholic Church established The Holy Office or the Congregation of the Inquisition. The goal of this institution, made up of six cardinals, was to get rid of heretics or those whose beliefs did not match the Church's, and fight the spread of Protestantism and other challenges to the Church's authority. Bishops and even cardinals were summoned before the group. Galileo, the Italian astronomer, was tried and condemned to house arrest in 1633 because he published findings that supported the Copernican view that Earth revolved around the Sun, even after the pope told him not to.

Censorship was one method the Church used to stop the spread of beliefs it considered heretical. Here a Dominican friar oversees the burning of books the Church did not approve of. The wording on the banner reads, "One God, One Faith, One Baptism."

The Trial

Inquisitors came under the direct control of the pope. Most were Franciscans or Dominicans because they were highly trained in theology and had given up worldly things. They even had the power to excommunicate royalty. Two inquisitors were in charge of each trial. They traveled to an area and announced that all guilty people should present themselves. Easier penalties were given to those who came forward voluntarily. After allowing a month for an accused person to confess, the inquisitors went ahead with a trial. Both clergy and lay people considered the verdict. Testimony of two witnesses was enough for a guilty judgment. For those who confessed or were found guilty, their sentences could be a public whipping, a fine, or penance, where the guilty might have to go on a pilgrimage. Serious cases were sent to prison, sometimes for life, or burned at the stake.

Witches

Witches were widely hunted throughout Europe in the 1500s, especially in Protestant countries. The pope had linked witchcraft with heresy, but the Inquisition largely ignored it in Spain and Italy. The Spanish Inquisition even set 1,500 accused witches free because of flawed evidence. Trials did take place in England, France, Germany, and Scotland. Those accused of being witches were usually older women, particularly if they used herbal remedies and potions. Some people saw signs of witchcraft if a

Forbidden Books

The Catholic Church published an Index of Forbidden Books in 1559. These were books Catholics were forbidden to read because they were considered harmful to the faith or one's morals. The list also included scientific works the Church disagreed with. A Catholic who read, sold, or passed on any literature on the list without special permission was excommunicated. The list continued in existence with new titles added and old ones removed until it was finally abolished in 1966.

Spanish heretics were executed in public ceremonies called an auto-da-fe, like this one in Madrid. The ceremony could involve burning the condemned person at the stake.

woman had a pet or if she had a mark on her skin that when pricked caused no pain. Victims were tortured until they confessed and then put in prison, exiled, or executed.

War and Religion

During the Renaissance, people's convictions about religious beliefs were strong. Religious differences often lead countries to go to war with one another, and also led to civil wars inside a country.

Huguenot Wars

France fought eight civil wars between the Catholics and Protestant Huguenots from 1562 to 1598. Many prominent French citizens had become Huguenot, but the monarchy remained Catholic. Sometimes the Huguenots were tolerated and at other times they were persecuted. In 1598 the French king issued the Edict of Nantes, giving Huguenots religious freedoms. Later kings ignored the edict and it was revoked in 1685.

Catholic Spain

Catholic Spain controlled the Netherlands, but Protestantism gained a following there during the Reformation. In 1567 a group of Dutch nobles rebelled against their Catholic rulers. Protestant England helped the Dutch in their rebellion against Spain. Spain and England fought against one another because one of Spain's goals was to return England to Catholicism. The Spanish Armada, a large fleet of Spanish war ships, attempted to invade England but was defeated in 1588. Many Armada ships were wrecked off the coast of Ireland on their dangerous voyage back to Spain. After a long war, the Netherlands eventually gained independence from Spain in 1648.

The Battle of Lepanto off the coast of Greece saw the Christian navies of Spain, Venice, and Genoa defeat the Ottoman navy's attempt to invade Cyprus in 1571. The allies captured more than 100 Ottoman galleys or ships and freed thousands of Christian slaves.

Muslim Pressure

The Muslim Ottoman Empire waged war to expand its territories. In 1526 the Ottoman army conquered much of Hungary, a Roman Catholic nation. The Holy Roman Empire, faced with this Muslim rival on its eastern border, feared that it would be invaded next. Christians fought to hold the city of Vienna, Austria in 1529 against the Ottomans, and successfully defended the Christian island of Cyprus from an Ottoman invasion in 1571.

Thirty Years' War

In 1618 conflict broke out in the Holy Roman Empire that eventually involved most of western and northern Europe until peace was declared in 1648. The Thirty Years' War was caused by antagonism between Protestants and Catholics, and between the kings and princes of these opposing religions. On October 24, 1648 the Peace of Westphalia was signed to end the war. Each state within the Empire was allowed independence, and the religion of the state was to be determined by the religion of its prince, whether he was Catholic, Calvinist, or Lutheran. If the prince changed his religion he had to give up his lands. The war put an end to the ideal of a group of Christian nations existing peacefully together and united under the supreme authority of one pope and one emperor.

A steel helmet of French or Italian origin from the 16th century. This type of helmet is called a burgonet. The front face cover is called a buffe, which could be opened up in some helmets. The comb on top strengthens the helmet and helps protect the head.

Weapons of War

At the start of the Renaissance, the longbow and crossbow were the main weapons used by foot soldiers. Groups of men armed with pikes, long poles with a sharpened end, held off knights on horseback. After the arrival in Europe of gunpowder in the 1200s, cannons were later developed that shot stones or steel balls to break down castle and city walls. Rifles that shot bullets could now penetrate a knight's armor, but strengthening that armor to resist bullets made it too thick and heavy to wear, so soldiers now wore only a chest plate and helmet.

Rebuilding and Renewing

Religious belief remained strong at the end of the Renaissance. Churches expressed their enthusiasm and devotion by rebuilding and renewing themselves. This resulted in a new and dramatic style of art and architecture.

Baroque Style

A new style in the arts called the Baroque developed in the late 1500s. It arose out of renewed religious enthusiasm all over Europe. The Baroque was a dramatic style. Painters such as Peter Paul Rubens, Rembrandt, and Caravaggio painted intensely emotional subjects. They used strong colors and a sharp contrast between light and shade. They wanted to engage viewers with exciting action. Music was elaborate and vividly expressive too. A new musical form developed that used solos, a large chorus, and many instruments to tell a religious story in a dramatic way. In architecture, the Baroque featured the use of curves rather than rectangles. It included intricate, twisting columns and lots of ornate painting and sculpture for decoration.

St. Peter's Basilica

Although work on this most famous of Catholic churches in Rome had begun decades earlier, finishing the basilica in the Baroque style became vitally important as a statement about the future of the Catholic Church. The basilica was consecrated in 1626 and became the center of Roman Catholic worship in the world. St. Peter's can hold up to 60,000 people.

The Swiss Guard maintains security in St Peter's Square and basilica in Rome. Swiss soldiers became permanent personal bodyguards for the pope in 1506 by agreement between Pope Julius II and Swiss government officials.

Protestant Churches

The newly–established Protestant faiths needed their own places of worship. Protestant churches and cathedrals were constructed all over Europe. In London, England, a great fire in 1666 destroyed the old cathedral. The city commissioned Christopher Wren to design a new one. Wren used the Baroque style in his design, which was approved in 1675.

Religious Freedom

Rebuilding for some religious groups meant leaving their homeland to find another place to live where they could practice their beliefs freely and without being persecuted. Many went to North America, searching for a safe place in which to practice their own religions. Puritans and Quakers left England because they wanted more reform in the Church of England. Catholics left England because it had become Protestant. Huguenots fled persecution in France for England, America, or the Netherlands. And Jews from throughout Europe left for the Americas to find a new life.

The pulpit, where a minister stands and preaches, in St. Katherine's church in Deggendorf, Germany. It shows the Baroque style of elaborate decoration.

The Church of England

When Henry VIII made himself head of the Church in England, he took away the pope's power to control it. His daughter, Mary I, a Catholic, gave that power back to the pope. In 1559 Queen Elizabeth I restored the independence of the Church of England from Rome. Parliament passed the Act of Supremacy which established Elizabeth as the head of the Church, forbade Catholic services, allowed priests to marry, and removed relics from churches. She also approved a new prayer book that the Church was to use.

Missionaries

Missionaries from both the Catholic and Protestant faiths went to other parts of the world to spread their beliefs.

The Mission

A missionary is someone sent, by their church, on a mission to another country, to preach their faith and convert others to Christianity. Missionaries were willing to travel to unknown lands and face harsh conditions. They believed it was their duty to teach their Christian faith to as many people throughout the world as possible. They also taught natives how to read and write. Catholic missionaries began spreading their faith to the new lands almost as soon as they were discovered. Franciscan and Dominican monks set up mission churches throughout South America and Mexico during the Spanish conquest of the region. The Jesuits were active missionaries. Francis Xavier, a Jesuit missionary born in Spain, established many missions in Asia. He was sent to convert people in Portuguese-controlled territory of India in 1542 and established a college in Goa to train priests. He then preached in Japan and by 1600 had converted as many as 300,000 people to Christianity. The Catholic Church declared him a saint in 1622.

Missionaries started coming to North America in the 1600s. Jean de Brébeuf, a French Jesuit missionary, set up the first Jesuit mission to the Huron Indians in 1626 on Georgian Bay in Lake Huron, Canada. The Franciscan, Louis Hennepin, founded a mission for the Iroquois Indians in 1676 in what is today Kingston, Ontario.

Father Louis Hennepin celebrates mass in the wilderness. Around 1680, while exploring the upper Mississippi Valley, he was captured by Sioux Indians and held for several months before returning to Canada in 1681.

Overseas Missions

In 1622, Pope Gregory XV started the Sacred Congregation for the Propagation of the Faith to provide a library for research and a school for training priests and missionaries. It assigned territories to missionaries and handled Church matters overseas. The Foreign Missionary Society of Paris, established in 1663, was set up to train local people to convert others in Vietnam, Thailand, Cambodia, and Laos.

Protestant Missionaries

Protestantism expanded as its followers moved overseas. As Protestants settled in North America, they became interested in the native population. John Eliot went from England to America in 1631. He became a missionary to the Indians in Massachusetts and learned their language, translating the Bible for them so that they could read it for themselves. He also organized a village of Indian converts near Boston in 1651. Thomas Mayhew, also from England, settled on Martha's Vineyard in 1641. He learned the native language from a Wampanoag native and in return taught him English and the beliefs of Christianity. His son continued the mission work so that by 1652, there were 283 converts and a school for native children.

A Jesuit missionary of the mid 1600s preaches to the native people in the Catholic colony of New France, today part of Canada. Jesuits set up many mission towns from the St. Lawrence River west to the Great Lakes to convert the native people.

Martyrs

Some early missionaries became martyrs, which means they suffered and died for their religion. Iroquois Indians captured Father Jean de Brébeuf and seven other missionaries from their Huron mission because the rival native peoples were at war with one another. The missionaries were tortured and killed in 1649. The Catholic Church later declared these men, known as the Jesuit North American Martyrs, to be saints, with a feast day on October 19.

Further Reading and Web Sites

Quigley, Mary. *The Renaissance*, Heinemann, 2003

Cole, Alison. *Eyewitness: Renaissance.* Dorling Kindersley, 2000

Langley, Myrtle. *Eyewitness: Religion.* Dorling Kindersley, 1996

Mason, Antony. *Everyday Life in Renaissance Times.* Minnesota: Smart Apple Media, 2006

Teacher Oz's Kingdom of History, Renaissance: www.teacheroz.com/renaissance.htm
Renaissance Connection: www.renaissanceconnection.org

Glossary

altarpiece Painted and decorated panel or wall behind an altar

bishopric The office of bishop

bubonic plague Deadly disease caused by a bacterium carried by rats

classical To do with ancient Greece and Rome and its language and arts

clergy Priests and other professional members of a church

convert Change; to turn someone from one religion to another

heretic Person who maintains beliefs contrary to the official views of a church

Holy Roman Emperor Elected leader of the Holy Roman Empire that controlled Germany and many other surrounding territories

horizontal Level with the ground

humanism Belief in the value of humans and the achievements of Greeks and Romans from their classical periods

indulgence A pardon for sins committed

lay Not part of the clergy

missionary Person sent on a mission by a church, often to teach or to convert someone to their own religion

monastery Place where monks or nuns lived to follow religious rules

Papal States Regions in Italy in 755-1870 under the domain of the pope

perspective Appearance of buildings or objects relative to each other

piazza Large square in the center of a city or town

pilgrimage Journey to a holy place, often in a foreign land

predestined Determined in advance by God

sacraments Christian ceremonial practices

seminary Institution to train priests

tax Compulsory payment to the government to raise revenue

Index

Printed in China — CT